THE
GHOSTLY TALES
OF
PHOENIX

Published by Arcadia Children's Books
A Division of Arcadia Publishing
Charleston, SC
www.arcadiapublishing.com

Spooky America is a trademark of Arcadia Publishing, Inc.

First published 2024

Manufactured in the United States

Designed by Jessica Nevins
Images used courtesy of Shutterstock.com; p. 34 You Touch Pix of EuToch/
Shutterstock.com; p. 46 Thomas Trompeter/Shutterstock.com.

ISBN 978-1-4671-9760-1

Library of Congress Control Number: 2023950131

Notice: The information in this book is true and complete to the best of our knowledge. It is offered without guarantee on the part of the author or Arcadia Publishing. The author and Arcadia Publishing disclaim all liability in connection with the use of this book.

Spooky America

THE
GHOSTLY TALES
OF
PHOENIX

STACIA DEUTSCH

Adapted from Haunted Phoenix By Debe Branning

arcadia
CHILDREN'S BOOKS

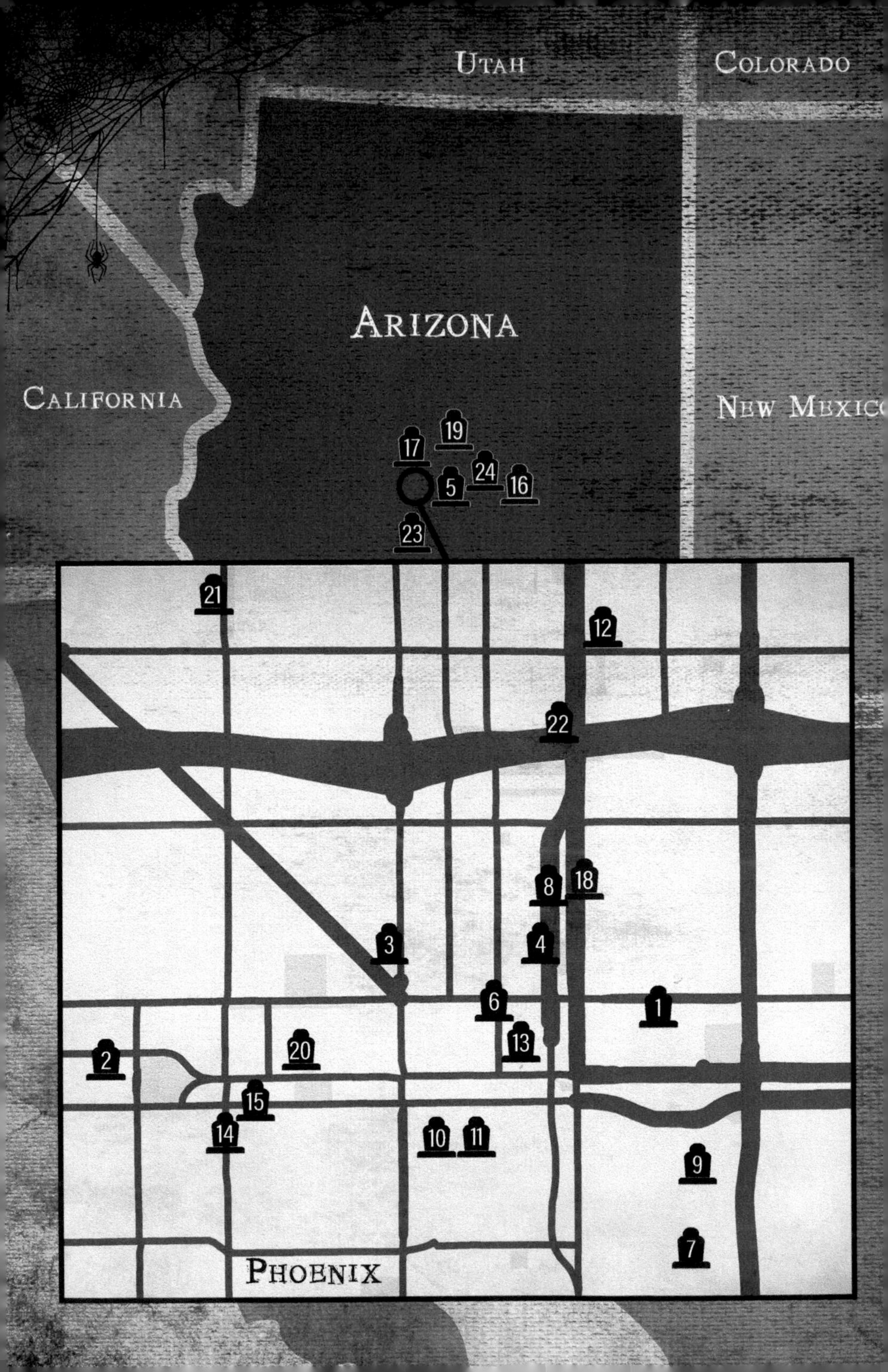
Utah
Colorado
Arizona
California
New Mexico
19
17
24
5
16
23
21
12
22
8
18
3
4
6
1
13
2
20
15
14
10
11
9
7
Phoenix

Table of Contents & Map Key

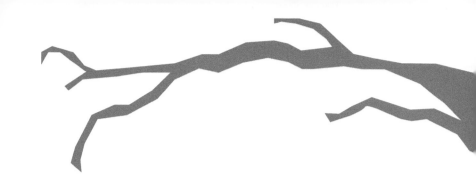

Welcome to Spooky Phoenix!

When you think of Phoenix, Arizona, you probably think of cacti and sunshine. Maybe Spring Training, if you love baseball. But there's much more to the "Valley of the Sun" than major league sports and rugged desert beauty. In the dark of night, Phoenix is also known for its ghosts!

In 1867, Jack Swilling, a Confederate

veteran of the Civil War, was traveling through the Salt River Valley. He was looking for good land to farm and found it on the ruins of a former Hohokam civilization. The Hohokam were an Indigenous tribe that lived in the area from about 200–1400 CE. Scientists aren't sure why, but they ultimately abandoned their settlement.

Jack Swilling told others to meet him there, and soon, a small community developed. The name "Phoenix" referred to a mythical bird that could die, rise from the ashes, and come back to life again. The new town was going to rise from the ruins of the past.

Phoenix became official on May 4, 1868, and Swilling was the first postmaster. The town grew quickly, and the arrival of the railroad in 1880 sped up that growth. People came and local businesses and industry took off. Cotton, cattle, citrus, copper, and climate were known locally as the "Five Cs" that made Phoenix great.

On February 14, 1912, Arizona became the forty-eighth state, and Phoenix became its official capital. In the 1930s, Phoenix adopted the nickname "The Valley of the Sun" to help boost tourism and bring people to the city. The nickname must have worked! By the year 2000, Phoenix had become one of the largest cities in the United States, with more than three million people calling it home.

But life wasn't *always* sunny in the Valley of the Sun. In fact, with so much rapid growth and expansion, the booming city had its fair share of tragedy, accidents . . . and even murder. To this day, some believe the restless spirits of those early pioneers and settlers still haunt the city's historic buildings, streets, and cemeteries. Just like the Phoenix bird, these ghosts rise from the dead to tell their stories.

Arizona State Capitol

Central District

ST. MARY'S BASILICA
231 North Third Street

St. Mary's Basilica, also called Church of the Immaculate Conception of the Blessed Virgin Mary, is the oldest Catholic community in Phoenix. The parish started before they had a building, but on June 24, 1881, a simple adobe church was dedicated and became the home of the parish. However, the parish soon outgrew that building, and it also needed major repairs.

It was torn down, and a beautiful new church was built on the same spot.

The church is an example of Mission Revival design with a Romanesque-style interior. It was hailed as an architectural masterpiece. There are four domes that transfer the weight of the roof to pillars. The center dome is topped with beautiful stained glass. Two bell towers house four bells, which ring daily. Today, St. Mary's Basilica is surrounded by skyscrapers; it is a bit of history hidden in the modern city.

On August 18, 1893, a man witnessed something incredible near the basilica. He kept silent about what he had seen until he met another man who had experienced the same thing the following night! Knowing he wasn't the only one who'd seen the bizarre occurrence, the man knew it was time to tell everyone what had happened.

"In the archway stood two female figures clad in white; they didn't look shadowy as ghosts are supposed to appear, but there was a strange plainness of an outline—luminous and uncanny. I could see their arms distinctly and their feet seemed to be incased in white slippers. Their hands were also unnaturally visible. . . . Strangest and most horrible of all, both of the figures were headless. Badly scared as I was, I remember I thought they resembled those mannequins used in a dressmaker's shop."

The second man reported that he had seen the exact same thing: two headless spirits standing in the archway!

After that, the man who had seen them first

refused to walk on the same side of the street as the church. He didn't want to chance running into those headless ghostly bodies ever again!

ARIZONA STATE CAPITOL
1700 WEST WASHINGTON STREET

The State Capitol building was built before Arizona even became a state. In fact, the building was erected to prove that the Arizona Territory was *ready* to become a state.

The capitol was designed by James Riely Gordon, who wanted it to be big, like the United States Capitol in Washington, DC. But there wasn't enough money. In the end, the building was smaller and made of local materials. Still, it was beautiful with impressive granite stone and hints of copper.

As the city and state's populations grew,

so did the capitol building. In 1918, and again in 1938, expansions were added. A tower was built in 1974. The dome was replaced with all copper and topped with a weathervane called Winged Victory. The Arizona State Capitol is now listed in the National Register of Historic Places, and the 1901 portion of the capitol is maintained by the Arizona Capitol Museum. It was in this older section of the building that a historian reported an "interesting energy."

On May 7, 1912, workmen were doing maintenance on the outside of the building. Inside, about one hundred and fifty people were working or discussing laws that would shape the new state. Clerks in the surveyor general's office labored quietly in their world of maps and land records.

Just before noon, violence interrupted the peaceful setting. Downstairs, near the east entrance, Frank Coffman barged in and shot the chief surveyor general clerk, Granville Malcolm Gillett. Coffman was convinced that Gillett had cheated him in a land deal and wanted revenge. His revenge complete, Coffman stepped back and shot himself, too.

Some say the spirits of these two men are the source of the "interesting" energy that the historian felt. Even more than a century later, they seem unable to resolve their dispute.

Another ghost is known to roam the halls of the Arizona State Capitol. Fifteenth governor, Wesley Bolin, was elected in 1977 and died a few months later from a heart attack. He was in his office at the time, and apparently his ghost is still on the job. It's thought that some of his ashes were scattered in the rose gardens, which is why the flowers continue to be stunningly beautiful!

LUKE-GREENWAY AMERICAN LEGION POST 1

364 NORTH SEVENTH AVENUE

The American Legion is a veterans' organization that welcomes those who have served in all branches of the United States Armed Forces. Since 1919, the organization has provided services and programs for veterans and the communities they live in.

American Legion Post 1 in Phoenix was named after Frank Luke, Jr. In 1939, the Frank Luke Jr. Post 1 and the John C. Greenway Post 50 merged to become the Luke-Greenway American Legion Post 1.

The combined post needed a building, and an old ostrich farm along Seventh Avenue and Polk Street in Central Phoenix filled the bill. The post started as a small place, but over the years, rooms were added to provide more space. Even though the building was modernized, the interior feels like a 1960s time warp. Perhaps the entire place is caught in the past, haunted by the ghost of the former caretaker.

John Lay, his wife, and their two children lived on the site in a basement apartment for several years. The apartment was located below the stage, where performances were held, and the family entered through a passageway in the former orchestra pit. Lay loved his job, and, after he passed away, the staff and members of the American Legion reported that his ghost was still living there.

"We often feel he is there keeping watch over things," a dedicated volunteer proclaimed. "We sense him in the building when we open the doors in the morning. Once we ventured down below to the old apartment and found a folder of the history of the post lying on top of some old boxes. None of us would have placed it there. Nobody had ever seen it before—or knew it even existed! It was as though John Lay sensed we needed the information and wanted us to find it."

Another time, there was a fire, and the fire department was shocked at what they found. A window, just above the fire, had not exploded from the heat, even though it should have. Stacks of papers were also stored in the room just on the other side of the wall near the window. Had the fire reached those papers, the entire building would have gone up in flames. But for some unexplainable reason, the fire had not spread.

The members of the post believe John Lay was watching over the building during the fire, as he always did. He was obviously a dedicated employee in life—*and* in death.

YMCA
350 FIRST AVENUE

Phoenix's first YMCA (Young Men's Christian Association) was opened in 1892 on the ground floor of a two-story building at First and Washington Streets. The YMCA was created to help young men who had "lost their way" and needed a clean place to bathe and sleep. This building served Phoenix for almost twenty years.

In 1911, a new facility was built and featured a gymnasium, a swimming pool, club rooms, and several residences. The building had three floors, but it was designed so that the roof could be raised to add additional floors if needed. A fourth floor was added to house troops passing through Phoenix during World War II.

After the war, the YMCA director proposed

constructing a bigger building with a more modern look. In 1952, the new downtown building opened, but a ghost from the old location moved right in.

On December 17, 1946, Quanah F. Parker, a radio ad salesman for KPHO, was found dead in his room at the old building from self-inflicted wounds. He was thirty-nine years old.

People have spotted the salesman's ghost repeatedly at the new building. Employees and visitors to the YMCA often see an apparition of a spooky specter in the hallways. Perhaps, having lost his way in life, Parker's spirit still needs a clean place to lie down in eternal sleep?

S'EDAV VA'AKI MUSEUM
(FORMERLY KNOWN AS PUEBLO GRANDE
MUSEUM AND ARCHAEOLOGICAL PARK)

4619 EAST WASHINGTON STREET

The S'edav Va'aki Museum is located on a 1,500-year-old archaeological site from the Hohokam culture.

It is believed that the Hohokam settled in this area around 450 CE and abandoned it a thousand years later, but no one knows why they left. The site is huge. It's the largest preserved archeological site within Phoenix and holds many mysteries.

One thing is clear, though: the Hohokam were innovators in farming. Their irrigation canals were preserved at the historic site, even as the city was built on their ruins.

But what happened to the people is not

the *only* mystery. There is a maze on the site that may have been considered a sacred place. Fascinating artifacts were found within the maze, leading archaeologists to believe the space was used for feasts and secret activities. In a couple of places, there are large, oval-shaped depressions in the ground. Archeologists believe these are courts for a ball game. It's known that early people living in the area loved ball games, but no one knows what the rules were. Experts think it was a cross between baseball and soccer, with a rubber ball and a stone hoop, but the experts also disagree about the game. Some think it was a large ball and some say it was smaller. Some experts even say that the losing team might have lost their lives!

The ruins of Pueblo Grande may not be known for ghost sightings, but locals still believe it is a *very* spiritual place. When you visit, be sure to walk around quietly. If you listen to the wind, you may hear the voices of the past, whispering you their stories ... and beware, if a spirit asks you to join them in a ball game, play hard. You definitely need to win.

FIRST BAPTIST CHURCH
302 WEST MONROE STREET

Built in 1929, Phoenix's historic and beautiful First Baptist Church is known to have its fair share of "spiritual" activity. An architectural work of art, the original building was designed in Italian Gothic style with stone columns, arched doorways, and other more modern details mixed in. As more and more people settled in Phoenix, the building became too small for its nearly two-thousand-member congregation. In time, the congregation moved to a new building in the suburbs, leaving the old building empty for decades.

Then, one February morning in 1984, the old church caught on fire.

A passing taxi driver reported the fire at 5:10 a.m. Only thirteen minutes later, most of the roof of the sanctuary had collapsed. It was an hour and twenty-nine minutes before the fire was contained. In the end, all that was left was a shell of the majestic building.

The building should have been empty, but was it?

Reports said that a man named "Wolf" was inside and died in the fire.

Before the fire, a group of homeless had moved in. The fire sent them scrambling for safety. No injuries were reported. Eleven people who had been living in the building were interviewed by local police. Some said "Wolf" was last seen going down to the basement to grab some of his belongings. They asked what had happened to him.

No one knew.

The question remains: Did someone die in the fire? Or not?

Years later, the shell of the burned-out building was still standing. Local artist, Robert John Miley, converted some space there into a studio. He'd been exploring various hidden alcoves within the building when he saw a small child with golden curls. Dressed in a fancy party dress and black patent leather shoes, she reminded him of the famous child actress, Shirley Temple. For a moment, Miley wondered how the little girl was able to enter his studio. Had he left the door unlocked? Where were the girl's parents? Had she accidentally wandered away from a celebration of sorts? Before he was able to ask where she'd come from, she disappeared.

Perhaps the young girl was one of the parish members who used to attend church here? Or maybe she died long ago and still haunts the building where her funeral was held? Either way, if you visit, keep a close watch. You might just see the Abbey's "Shirley Temple" for yourself.

GEORGE WASHINGTON CARVER MUSEUM AND CULTURAL CENTER

415 EAST GRANT STREET

The George Washington Carver Museum and Cultural Center was once the home of the Phoenix Union Colored High School. In 1926, it was a segregated school for Black students in the area. In 1943, the name of the school was changed to George Washington Carver High School, though it remained segregated.

Unfortunately, it was built on the site of a former trash dump surrounded by small factories and warehouses. Phoenix physicians worried that the site was contaminated and might cause students to get sick.

In 1953, when an Arizona court ruled against the school, the students were moved to other local high schools, and in 1954, George Washington Carver High School was shut down. In 1991, former students of the school came together and fought for it to be listed in the National Register of Historic Places. The property now serves as a museum and cultural center.

When the property was first under construction back in 1925, a caretaker house was built on site. It's said that the spirit of the caretaker is still there today. Many people claim to have experienced a male presence on the school grounds, but they say the spirit is protective, not angry. When they try to find out if the man is real, there's never anyone there.

George Washington Carver once said: "Anything will give up its secrets if you love it enough." The past students at the high school loved their building enough to make sure it was a protected historical site. It seems that the old caretaker continues to love the place, too.

What other secrets does the old high school hold? Only the ghosts know for sure!

WESTWARD HO HOTEL
618 NORTH CENTRAL AVENUE

Located at Central and Fillmore Streets, the luxurious Westward Ho opened its doors in November 1928. Until 1960, it was the tallest building in Phoenix, and it was popular! It was the place to see and be seen until it closed its doors in April 1980. According to some locals, it is *still* the place to see and be seen . . . by ghosts!

Many famous people stayed at the hotel, from presidents and actors to musicians and gangsters, including John F. Kennedy, Ronald Reagan, Paul Newman, Elizabeth Taylor, Shirley Temple, the Marx Brothers, Irving Berlin, Duke Ellington, Bugsy Siegel, and Al Capone, among many others. Amelia Earhart even stayed at the Westward Ho before her plane mysteriously vanished in 1937.

But things at the Westward weren't all glitz and glamour. In September 1941, the Westward Ho was the scene of a robbery. Two bandits, one of them disguised with theatrical makeup, held up the Westward Ho Hotel and escaped with more than $300 (a little over $6,000 in today's money). In 1947, a guest went to jail for firing a gun and leading police on a chase through the hallways.

In 1958, jewels were stolen from the hotel vault. There is a story that a young boy, about twelve years old at the time, witnessed someone get out of a big black car and dump two suitcases into the bushes. The boy took the suitcases home, and when he opened them—to his surprise—there were the jewels! The kid didn't want to get in trouble, so he buried the bags, making a note to himself about where to find them later.

According to the story, the city of Phoenix paved over the spot and made a road.

Years later, in October 1975, a man claimed to be that child. He told someone who then told the police that the gems were still in the area. The details seemed to match up. Phoenix police went on a treasure hunt looking for the $53,000 of stolen jewels, digging up the street. However, they didn't find anything.

In September 2001, psychic Jackie Kranz, along with ghost hunter and author of *Haunted Phoenix*, Debe Branning, were invited by the Historical Committee Team of the Westward Ho Hotel to take a tour of the building with paranormal investigator, Earling Eaton.

Jackie's first job was at the hotel when she was a teenager, and she was excited to explore.

When Earling opened the door to the basement, they found tunnels that once ran under busy Central Avenue to a parking lot. The tunnels had collapsed during the construction of the Phoenix Valley Metro Light Rail, so there wasn't much to explore down there. They also went into the dressing rooms and lockers where staff prepared for their workday.

Unfortunately, they didn't see or feel any ghosts that day. But that doesn't mean ghosts weren't there!

Two months later, the MVD Ghostchasers held a paranormal workshop at the Westward Ho, which Jackie attended. They called themselves MVD Ghostchasers because so many in the group once worked for the State of Arizona Motor Vehicle Division. Several of the investigators sensed there was once a brutal fight or accident in the penthouse area on the fifteenth floor, known as the Garden Deck. As one of the investigators walked through the spot, he suddenly grabbed his cheek. He said it felt like he walked into the middle of a fistfight and was slapped by some unseen force. He had to sit down and catch his breath. Others described the area as a sad, depressing space and avoided the spot.

Jackie said, "I had a very uneasy feeling exploring the Garden Deck, too. I wanted to go back downstairs."

The hotel later underwent a renovation and was converted into an apartment building. The old Thunderbird Ballroom was split into two floors and converted into thirty-two modern apartments.

After moving in, residents reported that a ghostly dancer, a "Lady in a Red Dress," was still in the building. They'd see her twirling through their rooms as though the dance floor had never been removed. Sometimes, they'd even hear the big-band music of Red Nichols and his Five Pennies. Red and the band often stayed and played for guests at the Westward Ho in the 1940s.

Other residents reported strange things at the apartments. One said their kitchen utensils moved around without being touched (at least not by human hands!). Another said that a stove turned on by itself, and they often heard large boxes being moved at night.

A former female security guard said she once went to check out a call from the thirteenth floor. When she tried to leave the elevator, her muscles froze and she couldn't move. It was as if a ghost was holding her in place.

There is another story of an older man who lived on the third floor. After he died, a new tenant moved in, but she said the ghost of the old man was still there. She'd find him sitting on the edge of her bed. He obviously didn't want to get off his bed even though he was dead!

One of the greatest myths about the Westward Ho involves the famous mobster Al Capone. It's believed that his car—filled with cash and jewels—is buried under rubble in the old basement. The famous gangster used to stay at the hotel in the late 1920s through 1931. This was during Prohibition, when the manufacture and sale of alcoholic beverages was illegal in the United States. At the time, some hotels had secret bars that were not on the map, called speakeasies. Al Capone liked the speakeasy at the Westward Ho.

The basement had a large underground parking garage, and some say Al Capone's car was there when the basement collapsed in 1935. Capone was already in prison, so maybe that's where he hid some of his money, hoping he'd get out and come back for it. No one knows for sure, but an older resident swore the story was true.

Perhaps Capone's restless spirit occasionally drops in to look for his missing treasures?

Now, since the hotel has been turned into apartments, there are no ghost hunts or tours available. You can visit only if you have family or friends who live there—that is, unless you, like Al Capone or the Lady in the Red Dress, just so happen to be haunting the place . . . .

Phoenix Union Station

Old Warehouse District

PHOENIX UNION STATION
401 SOUTH FOURTH AVENUE

In 1923, the Phoenix Union Station was completed. It was an architectural marvel. There was a central two-story waiting room connecting two long wings that had low arches, a red-tiled roof, curved gables, massive pillars, and decorative molding. The waiting room had a high ceiling with beams, wooden furnishings, and chandelier light fixtures.

Though the building is no longer a train station, it still has the original beautiful tile in the bathroom and carved oak refreshment counter. The ticket booths and luggage carts also remain.

At its peak, immediately after World War II, the Phoenix Union Station would see as many as eighteen trains a day. Special occasions were celebrated there, and thousands of people made happy memories within those walls.

But ... it wasn't all happy.

In 1931, the "trunk murderess," Winnie Ruth Judd, packed bits and pieces of her former roommates into two large trunks and a hatbox. She had them loaded onto the train as cargo.

Her murder spree began on the evening of October 16, 1931, when Winnie had an argument with her two best friends. All three of them liked the same married man. Winnie wanted to be his girlfriend so badly that she shot her friends and chopped them up. She, and the bodies in her luggage, were headed to Los Angeles.

When the train reached Los Angeles, Winnie went to get her trunks. A porter demanded a key to look inside. He thought the trunks contained illegal deer meat because they were leaking blood.

They caught her. The "trunk murderess" went to prison.

Today, Sprint Communications owns the building and stores equipment in the old train station. It's not the trunk victims they see, but rather, workers say they are haunted by a ghost called "Fred." The station's security guard/ maintenance man said, "Whenever you are up in the attic of the station, and you feel a tap on your shoulder, and you turn around to find no one is there—that is Fred!" Some maintenance workers and repairmen refuse to go into the attic alone.

The ghost has been known to open and close the heavy side gate or appear as a shadowy figure in a room. But just who is Fred? Is he a former railroad station employee? A train passenger who spent a lot of time at the train station?

Many paranormal investigators have tried to make their way into the buildings at the station, but they weren't able to get past the wire fence and barbed wire. However, a communications class from Scottsdale Community College was able to arrange a special tour of the train station. They wanted to study the huge wiring system in the station, as well as the amazing decor.

A group of female students went to use the ladies' room and were shocked when they discovered a man there. The students shrieked and ran out of the restroom. The instructor, another group of students, and the security guard ran into the ladies' room to confront the man. But there was no one there. The security guard declared, "Must have been Fred!"

Whoever Fred is, perhaps someday he'll catch a ghost train and make it to his final destination.

SANTA FE FREIGHT DEPOT
334 SOUTH FIFTH AVENUE

Near the Phoenix Union Station was the Santa Fe Freight Depot. Freight are goods or cargo carried by a large vehicle, like a truck or train. Erected in 1929, the building was where the offices for the managers and workers were found. For decades, the depot was a very busy place. Today, it serves as offices for Maricopa County.

Phoenix's "Hip Historian," Marshall Shore, had an office in a building across the street from the depot. (Keep reading for more on that haunted building!) Marshall ran his Haunted Phoenix bus tour business out of that space. One afternoon, a man who worked for the county spotted Marshall unloading his vehicle outside his office. He walked across the street, introduced himself to Marshall, and told him a ghost story. It went like this:

A few years ago, the man was working late when it started raining hard—the kind of storm that only comes along once every century. Water was rising fast and streets began to flood. The man still had a small project to finish and didn't live very far away, so he stayed at the office. All of a sudden, he heard what sounded like an old-fashioned typewriter, clicking and clacking in the distance. It sounded like an office clerk from the past, hurriedly typing up freight invoices for the old Santa Fe Depot.

The man looked everywhere, but couldn't find whoever, or whatever, was making the

sound. Suddenly, the clicking stopped. A wave of fear washed over the man, and he left the building as fast as he could.

Marshall Shore wrote down the story and has been telling it ever since.

I wonder if that ghostly freight clerk is still processing invoices, or if he has finally moved on to "retirement"?

THE ICEHOUSE
429 WEST JACKSON STREET

Before people had refrigerators and freezers in their homes, ice was stored at The Constable Ice and Fuel Company building (now known as the Icehouse). It was built in 1920 and still stands across the street from the Santa Fe Freight Depot.

Once the building was no longer needed for ice storage, the Phoenix Police Department used the space to store crime-scene evidence. The building was listed in the National Register of Historic Places on September 4, 1985, and today it serves as a cultural center that promotes the arts and humanitarian causes.

But what really lurks within the walls? Marshall Shore, whose office was in the basement of the Icehouse, invited Debe Branning and a friend on a tour of the place. They were interested in finding out if the Icehouse would be a good location to conduct a group paranormal investigation.

The tour began outside a storage shed where crime-scene evidence had been held. They didn't feel anything strange there, but once they got to the top floor of the main building, they felt a creepy heaviness in the air.

Debe's friend, Cindy, said it felt like something really bad had happened in the room. She raised her arms and announced that she felt a male energy. She wondered if maybe someone had died up there. A very dark and negative force lingered in the space. She didn't like it in there at all.

They got out quickly.

Another time, the Crossing Over Paranormal team, led by Jay and Marie Yates, investigated the Icehouse. They caught a lot of EVP (Electronic Voice Phenomenon) with their recorder and were able to capture voices from the past. When Marie felt like she was being pushed by invisible hands, Jay went on alone. He saw a shadow cross in front of a door frame, and then, the group began having a lot of otherworldly experiences.

The group heard knocks and bangs in response to questioning in the outside evidence room. They described the sound of screams and the sight of eerie shadows visible in the windows.

What do you think? Is it possible they were all spooked for no reason? Or, could the shadows, voices, and strange noises that lurk in the Icehouse serve as proof that ghosts are *real* . . . and not frozen in time?

The Orpheum Theater

CHAPTER 3

Phantoms of the Theater

PHOENIX THEATRE
1825 NORTH CENTRAL AVE

In the early 1920s, a theater troupe called the Phoenix Players performed all over town. Now, under the name The Phoenix Theatre Company, they are recognized as the oldest arts organization in Arizona. Their past includes playing in backyards and schools, but by 1952, they'd raised money for their own building. Still, even a new building can have old ghosts.

"Mr. Electric" is the best-known spirit that haunts their building. Imagine finding a little old man sitting on the flies (pipes) high above the stage, where the lights are hung. Mr. Electric really loves lighting, and sometimes he flickers the lights during a production. It's as if he puts on his own show whenever he's in the mood.

The "Tiny Dancer" is a spirit that first appeared in 2005, during a production of *A Chorus Line*. She's a petite ballerina who joins the cast as an extra dancer during big musical numbers.

A prankster ghost called the "Prop Master" frequents the prop room, where items used on stage are stored. He thinks it's hysterical to lock the stage crew in the prop room when they are in a hurry or when he has a different idea for how a show should run.

The ghost of "Light Board Lenny" is another playful spirit who has locked lighting technicians out of the lighting booth. Maybe he's working with Mr. Electric to take over the lights?

And lastly, there is "Poor Freddy." It's believed that Freddy is the ghost of an actor. After being fired from a show, he was killed in a bicycle accident on his way home. Freddy has a temper. He slams doors and throws items around, letting everyone know that he should have been the star!

Theaters are hives of activity, energy, and excitement. And it seems the ghosts of the

Phoenix Theatre don't want to give up being a part of that—even in the afterlife!

ORPHEUM THEATRE
203 WEST ADAMS STREET

Phoenix's elegant and enchanting Orpheum Theatre has been home to some incredible performances over the years, as well as some very ghostly guests!

Built in 1929 and known for its glitz, glamour, and lavish design, the theater promised to be "the most beautiful playhouse west of the Mississippi." Stepping inside the Orpheum was like being transported to another world. The exquisite theater boasted two thousand leather seats, lush flowers, a glimmering fountain, and hanging vines that made the space look more like an enchanted forest than a theater. Even the domed ceiling was a sight to behold, painted to look like an endless blue sky dotted with airy, light-filled clouds.

The theater was extremely successful for a few decades, beginning with traveling vaudeville shows that were part of the nationwide Orpheum Circuit. Vaudeville was a popular form of entertainment in the mid-1890s until the early 1930s that included comedy, musical, and performing animal acts. The theater played movies through the 1940s and 50s (and was renamed the Paramount Theatre during that time), but by the mid-1960s, the downtown scene began to shift. After changing owners several times and later falling into disrepair, the theater was sold to the City of Phoenix in 1984. The city began a thirteen-year, $14.5 million restoration project, and the new Orpheum reopened on January 28, 1997.

Today, most guests come to see plays and Broadway shows, but others visit the Orpheum on ghost tours.

One evening, Cindy Lee was attending a theater show with a group of her best friends. When Cindy went to the restroom, she saw a woman standing by herself near the back of the theater, dressed in a lovely old-fashioned gown and a large maroon hat. When Cindy approached the woman to ask who had made her dress, she was stunned to watch the lady suddenly vanish before her very eyes! Cindy is good at picking up ghost energy, and something told her the ghost's name was Maggie.

In June 2015, another paranormal team called FOTOS (Friends of the Other Side) did an investigation with Phoenix Ghost Tours. They encountered the same female spirit in the wide-brimmed hat. She was standing in the theater balcony. FOTOS leader Carolee Jackson picked up on the name "Maddie."

Was the woman's name Maddie or Maggie? Looking back at the old Phoenix census reports, it looks like the theater owner, Harold Nace, had a relative named Maggie Nace. Perhaps this is the same person?

Nobody really knows who Maddie/Maggie might be, but apparently, she has ghostly friends who also hang out at the Orpheum.

Carolee Jackson has seen an older man dressed in a white shirt with the sleeves rolled up, dark pants, and no tie or hat. He calls himself Gilbert and appears in a shadow form, sometimes known to follow the cleaning crew around the theater after the performances have ended and the crowds have gone home. (Perhaps he's checking to make sure they do a good job tidying up!)

Carolee has also sensed two young spirit boys playfully running across the lower seat aisles at the Orpheum when she was giving a ghost tour. Unfortunately (or maybe fortunately, depending how you feel about ghosts!), the boys disappeared as quickly as they appeared.

The stage also holds the energy of two men in a fistfight. The crashing and banging noises they make have even been recorded by a sound technician. One of the men might be the spirit of an orchestra drummer by the name of Fred Ice. He came to the theater one night, angry and emotional that his wife had died. He thought a doctor was to blame for her death, and that doctor was seeing a show at the Orpheum that night. It's unclear if the men really fought, but some locals believe Fred Ice was so angry that he left his energy in the building . . . for all eternity.

In 2018, Debe Branning was seeing a movie at the old theater, when her friend suddenly noticed a spirit hovering on the right side of the stage. This "Grey Lady" was a ghostly woman wearing a grayish floral dress. She swished her dress side to side and then suddenly disappeared, only to reappear a moment later on the *left* side of the stage! Debe and all her friends were shocked. They'd all seen her!

To keep the theater's ghosts company, there is apparently a "ghost cat" from the 1920s that hangs around. Back in 1929, workers named the cat "Tom" and welcomed it in the theater. Both actors and security guards claim they've heard purring, and some say they've even seen the ghostly cat knocking things off a table in the theater.

Debe likes to think that Tom has nine lives, just like the historic Orpheum Theater.

CHAPTER
4

Tales from the Crypt

AN ARIZONA TOMBSTONE RESCUE

The Pioneers' Cemetery Association (PCA) in Phoenix, Arizona, received a message. It wasn't a ghostly voice calling from beyond the grave, but rather a woman who had been out antique shopping in the northern part of the state. She had found an old tombstone monument in a store and wondered if the PCA could look up the names listed on the front. The woman wanted to know if the obelisk-shaped stone had come from a cemetery in Arizona. This was exactly the kind of thing that Debe Branning did with the PCA, so Debe decided to do a bit of research.

It turned out that the old monument belonged in the Pioneer & Military Memorial Park (a complex of several cemeteries). Mysteriously, the tombstone had been missing from the burial grounds for over seventy years! Though nobody knew how it had gone missing, one thing was certain: it was time to bring the large grave marker home.

Debe and her friend, Megan Taylor, headed to Mayer, Arizona, only to discover that the stone was too big to fit in the car. They needed a truck.

When they arrived at the antiques shop the next morning, this time in a truck with a hoist, they took a more careful look at the treasure. There were two names on the stone: M. J. Brady and Joe Brady.

Debe and Megan couldn't find out much about Joe Brady, but Debe discovered that M. J. Brady had worked at a grocery store in Phoenix. She also learned that before his body came to the cemetery, his corpse had been robbed! Mr. Brady kept the money he made from the store under his pillow at night. On the morning he died, his wife alerted the neighbors, and soon the house was filled with a small crowd. After the crowd left and the coroner had viewed the body, M. J. Brady's wife remembered the money her husband kept under his pillow. But when she looked for it, the money was gone!

Poor M. J. Brady had been robbed twice: once from his deathbed, and then from his gravestone! Only his spirit knows who is to blame!

HOHOKAM DIG:
THE REAL GHOSTS OF PIONEER & MILITARY MEMORIAL PARK

In 2010, the City of Phoenix outlined a plan for major underground storm sewer drain construction at the Pioneer & Military Memorial Park, which is a cemetery. Shortly after the digging began, historic Hohokam relics began to surface. (The Hohokam were Indigenous peoples who lived in the area between 200 and 1400 CE.) A group of archaeologists was sent to the site. They needed to gather the artifacts and take photographs before the sewer construction could continue. The archaeologists uncovered walls, doorways, steps, hearths, storage pits, holes for canopy poles, and lots of pot shards. They determined that twenty-two Hohokam dwellings, as well as an ancient burial ground, lay beneath the dead pioneers buried in the park.

Even though the archeological find was re-covered once the study was completed, the spirits and the lives of the Hohokam still remain.

One morning, Debe Branning was at the park doing volunteer work. She was cleaning up and found a piece of Hohokam pottery. Suddenly, it felt like someone pushed her from behind, and she almost tumbled into a burial plot! Luckily, she steadied herself, but her blue jeans had been ripped on the iron fence surrounding the plot.

Debe realized that she had angered the Hohokam spirits by removing the piece of pottery. In a quick move, she placed the shard back into the dirt where she had found it.

Debe had learned an important lesson: Never remove a piece of Hohokam pottery from a site ... that is, unless you're prepared to deal with the spooky consequences!

"SISTO": THE OLD GRAVEDIGGER OF THE PHOENIX CEMETERY

Most ghosts probably prefer to spend their afterlife among flowers and mowed lawns rather than weeds and discarded trash. However, the Loosely Cemetery, which is part of the Pioneer & Military Memorial Park, had been overrun by weeds, mesquite brush, and other desert plants for decades.

Sisto Lizarraga, who was Phoenix's official grave digger, finally decided to clean up. He and a team of four men pulled weeds and set back fifty-two tombstones that had either fallen or were leaning in the soft ground. Together,

Sisto and his team brought the cemetery back to life. (See what we did there?)

Though Sisto passed away many years ago, Debe Branning and her colleagues believe that his spirit still guards the cemetery. He protects the grounds and the cemetery residents from evil forces and visiting humans. That's probably why people have heard voices in the cemetery telling them to leave. Sisto obviously wants to make sure the grounds stay safe and beautiful for all time, ensuring that people buried there really can rest in peace.

And that's not the only strange thing going on. Work crews have noticed that trees have been trimmed and rocks have been carefully placed to mark a historic tombstone. The question is . . . placed by *whom*? Is this the work of the City of Phoenix landscapers? Or, could it be the spirit of Sisto, making sure the cemetery he loved is forever kept neat and tidy?

HUNT'S TOMB
625 NORTH GALVIN PARKWAY

Debe Branning remembers exploring the hiking trails at Papago Park and coming upon a large white pyramid, high above a hill, overlooking the Phoenix Zoo. When she learned that the pyramid was actually a *tomb* (that's right, a tomb overlooking a ZOO), she wanted to know more.

It didn't take Debe long to discover that the man with the pyramid-shaped tomb overlooking the Phoenix Zoo was none other than Arizona's first governor, George W. P. Hunt (1859-1934). The land belongs to the City of Phoenix and is in a secluded area of Papago Park. Buried with him are his wife, in-laws, daughter, and a son-in-law. Their resting place looks down into the zoo's antelope habitat.

George W. P. Hunt was born in Huntsville, Missouri, on November 1, 1859. His family moved west, and he spent his childhood in Globe, Arizona. Governor Hunt, who served seven terms in office, called himself the "Old Walrus."

Before he died, the governor chose a pyramid for his burial monument, a practice that the Ancient Egyptians are best known for. They believed that a pyramid represents the early, original mound from which the Earth was created. The pyramid's shape represents the descending rays of the sun, and the chambers at the top are intended to attract the sun god Ra on his journey across the sky. Ancient Egyptians also believed that a daily encounter with Ra would allow the dead to take on the role of the great sun god in the afterlife. Others say a pyramid acted like a machine that would resurrect the dead. So, what did George Hunt hope would happen to him once he was dead and buried?

George Hunt and his family traveled to Egypt in the 1930s to explore the great pyramids and monuments. When he learned about Ra and the mythology, he wanted his own pyramid.

Congress granted Hunt permission to build his thirty-foot-by-twenty-foot pyramid. It is covered with white polished tiles and can be seen from almost anywhere in Papago Park. As the eerie-looking mausoleum (an impressive, above-ground tomb used to store

the remains of people who have died) was being constructed, Governor Hunt was quoted as saying, "The people of this state have been good to me, and in my last sleep, I want to be buried so that I may, in my spirit, look over this splendid valley that in years to come will be a Mecca of those that love beautiful things and, in the state, where people rule."

Hunt's tomb is still one of Debe's favorite places to visit. The tomb is not only in a lovely location, but you never know if you'll see a ghost hanging around.

If you visit, be sure to tell Governor Hunt how much you enjoy the view. He'll be happy to hear it.

CHAPTER 5

Pioneer Living Museum

3901 WEST PIONEER ROAD

Just a quick thirty-minute car ride from downtown Phoenix, you'll find the Pioneer Living History Museum. The museum is a ninety-acre site that contains a nineteenth-century reconstructed town with some authentic buildings and others that are historically reproduced. Can you guess what else the museum site contains? If you guessed *ghosts*, you're on the right track!

As new homes and buildings were being built in the state, the Pioneer Arizona Foundation was worried. What would happen to the historic buildings? They didn't want them torn down, so to protect the past, the buildings were moved, and a nineteenth-century reconstructed town was created. The museum, with thirty historic buildings, opened in 1969.

Of course, some of the historic buildings came with pioneer spirits of the past. Paranormal teams, such as the MVD Ghostchasers, Arizona Desert Ghost Hunters, and Phoenix Arizona Paranormal Society (PAPS), have experienced unexplained phenomena during their investigations at the location—especially when the sun goes down. Let's meet some of the roaming spirits and ghosts who just weren't ready to leave their homes.

VICTORIAN HOUSE

John Marion Sears built the stately Victorian House in the early 1890s on his eighty-acre homestead in Phoenix. Apple, peach, pear, and almond orchards dotted the property. There was a pumphouse and windmill, and even a dairy.

Volunteers and guides who work in the building report hearing footsteps and having the sensation of being watched.

One paranormal investigator said, "We filmed an apparition moving from the main living room to the piano room. We also filmed a light moving in and out of the curtains as if it was trying to hide. A photograph of what appears to be a rod-shaped light was captured by the front porch. One of our team members had her pant leg pulled by an unseen force. A child's voice and woman's voice have both been recorded in the house, as well as a man saying, 'I'm tired.'"

And if you visit the house, you might want to bring a coat. One of the ghosts was recorded saying, "It's cold out here," even though it was the middle of summer . . .

Would you be nervous if a ghost said, "Hi"? It's happened at the museum, so you might want to wear your running shoes in case you decide to get out of there quickly!

FLYING V CABIN

The Flying V Cabin is originally from Young, Arizona, and was built around 1880. When you look closely, you'll see notched gun ports built in the walls for protection against attacks. These are holes in the walls that allowed the barrel of a gun to stick through. It meant whoever was in the cabin could fight off an attack. The cabin was once raided on July 17, 1883, during the Battle of Big Dry Wash—a battle between the US Army and members of the White Mountain Apache. Horses were stolen during the battle, but the house was not damaged.

The cabin is believed to have been built by John Tewksbury Sr., the head of the Tewksbury family. They were involved in a ten-year feud with another family in the area, the Grahams.

Members of both families were killed during the feud.

During the paranormal investigation, the word "weapon" was reportedly captured on an EVP. With the house's history, there are any number of ghosts who might be talking about weapons. If you visit the Pioneer Living Museum, listen carefully as those ghosts may have more to say. But are you scared about what you might hear?

ASHURST CABIN

Arizona's first senator, Henry Fountain Ashurst, grew up in this 1878 home. In 1968, it was moved piece by piece from Ashurst Springs to its current location at the Pioneer Museum, where it was restored to its former glory.

A paranormal investigator recalled that on one tour, "One of the SB7 Spirit Boxes captured a man saying, 'you're grumpy,' a female entity stating, 'a couple' after an investigator questioned 'how many spirits are here?' And, after being asked 'how are you?' in Spanish, a female voice said, 'I don't speak.'"

Sounds like plenty of ghosts hitched a ride with the cabin when it was moved to the museum...

MERRITT HOUSE

John and Emma Merritt had three children, two boys, Glenn and Melvin, and a daughter named Beryl. They moved to Arizona in 1920, where Beryl was born. This old house was hers until 2008, when she donated it to the museum.

"This was an interesting location," a paranormal investigator reported after touring the house. "A bathroom door opened on its own—hitting a member of the team as he felt an energy field pass through him. Doors on the dresser opened on their own. We were unable to photograph anything in the main bedroom at times. There were also the sounds of heels walking in this same main bedroom. We recorded an EVP of a man saying 'teapot' as we entered the kitchen area."

Perhaps one of the ghosts was hoping for a cup of tea?

NORTHERN HOME

The Northern Home was built around 1885 and moved to its present location from Nevada. A paranormal investigator reported that, "A tour guest was touched on the shoulder in the Northern Home. And we also received multiple SB7 Spirit Box responses including 'Get out,' and 'Don't talk like that.' After being asked if we were bothering the spirits inhabiting the home, a male stated his name was 'John.'"

The house was originally the home of Jeff D. Newman, his wife, and their eight children. So, who's John?

OPERA HOUSE

The Opera House, known as Howey Hall, originally served as a general store when it was built. Levi Bashford bought the building and, in 1882, he transformed into a theater. He remodeled the building, adding dressing rooms and installing upholstered chairs. There was even an ice-skating rink on the main floor. Many famous celebrities of the time performed there. However, in 1894, the Opera House was declared unsafe and eventually closed. When it was torn down, the bricks were numbered and used in an authentic reconstruction of the building. It looks exactly as it did in the late 1800s.

A Phoenix paranormal team, Arizona Desert Ghost Hunters, talked about their experience in the Opera House in 2004:

"A team member placed a digital recorder on a chair in front of the stage at the opera house. At 2:00 a.m. we reviewed the recorder. What we heard was astonishing. For over forty minutes, there was nothing but static on the recorder, then without warning, the group began to hear sounds of a loud train depot. The screeching of steel on steel, loud banging like cars being coupled and uncoupled, muffled voices and many other loud noises. That lasted for exactly twenty-one minutes, then there was only static noise again. Keep in mind the closest railroad tracks are almost twenty miles away."

Another team said, "A female entity has been documented several times on the stage, apparently performing, because EMF (Electric and Magnetic Field) levels rose and fell with the interaction of applause and cheering. After being asked 'Will you dance for us?' We captured a female stating, 'No one will see.' We also captured a female sadly sighing, and someone telling us to 'Sit down' as we walked into the building to investigate."

Sounds like performers, as well as audience members, are still showing up for shows at the Opera House.

ON THE ROAD

MVD Ghostchaser Gary Tone was once a Tempe, Arizona, police officer. He said that one night, while he was driving a prisoner to a facility just north of Phoenix, he noticed a gentleman on the right side of the roadway. He was wearing period clothing and a top hat, and he was carrying a satchel. Gary and the prisoner in his police car watched as the man ran across four lanes of traffic in the direction of the museum. The Pioneer Living Museum sits next to a former stagecoach route. Perhaps it's still a drop-off destination for some of its former passengers. Could they still be hoping to make it to their final destination?

If you get a chance to visit the Pioneer Living Museum, keep your eyes and ears peeled, as there are plenty of spirits around that make this site a very real ghost town!

Mysteries of the Underground

THE GOLD SPOT BOWLING ALLEY
621 NORTH CENTRAL AVENUE
(NO LONGER STANDING)

The former site of Phoenix's abandoned and long-forgotten bowling alley, the Gold Spot, might just be another location to test out your ghost-hunting radar. Built underground, below the Neilson Radio and Sporting Goods Building on Central Avenue and Pierce Street, the Gold

Spot opened in 1935 across from the Westward Ho Hotel (yes, the same spooky hotel from Chapter 1). It was hugely popular in the 1940s and in the years following World War II.

But by 1950, sadly, the Gold Spot's popularity had dwindled. The once-bustling bowling haven closed its doors forever and sat empty (and eerie) for more than forty years. In 1991, the building complex was demolished, and a few determined city explorers found their way into the subterranean site after spotting old skylights in the sidewalk that led them to the tunnels below the Westward Ho.

It's unclear whether the Gold Spot is home to any ghosts, but a creepy, abandoned, subterranean bowling alley sure seems like a good place to find them! After all, even the spirits can't resist a fun night of bowling (or should we say . . . *boo-ling*?) here and there!

In 2008, the last known access point to the

underground bowling alley was filled with concrete, burying the Gold Spot Bowling Alley and its secrets forever. But if you ever happen to be walking down North Central Avenue, keep your eyes open for the glass sidewalk panels, and your *ears* open for ghostly bowlers doing their best to get a strike!

PHOENIX'S BAT CAVE
3698–3694 East Colter Steet

Do you know about the Phoenix Bat Cave? This notorious but little-known place is at the end of a hidden asphalt pathway. The bat cave, which is actually a tunnel and part of an isolated canal system, is home to thousands of Mexican free-tailed bats that breed there every summer. In the evening, the bats take flight and zoom out of the tunnel, searching for small insects for dinner.

The origin of the canal dates back hundreds of years to the Hohokam people. Their irrigation ditches brought water from the river to irrigate their crops. Settlers used the traces of these ditches to shape the current canal system.

Check it out! The cave is just a quick walk along the canal path. You'll definitely have bragging rights if you're up for braving the bats. It's an incredible site to behold. And though bats aren't nearly as spooky (or vampiric) as they might seem in scary movies, you might want to bring some garlic along . . . just in case.

Haunted Mansions

EVANS HOUSE
1100 WEST WASHINGTON STREET

The Evans House, located near the Arizona State Capitol building, was built by Dr. John M. Evans in 1893. His offices were on the top floor. Because of the home's unique dome roof, it became known as "The Onion House." The unique house was listed in the National Register of Historic Places on September 1, 1976.

Dr. Evans moved out of the house in 1904. And, in 1908, Oscar Livingston Mahoney and his family moved into it. Oscar had served as a Confederate soldier in the Civil War and also as a county coroner. (A coroner is a public official who determines how people died.) Oscar's wife, Virginia, was one of only four women who had a license to practice medicine in the Arizona Territory.

Debe Branning and a friend decided to stop by the house after hearing rumors of its paranormal activity. There, they met Joseph Roth, who was happy to share stories of the strange goings-on.

Joseph told Debe and her friend that he had been working in the building when he walked out of his office to look for a file. A minute later, he returned and saw the maintenance man standing in front of his desk, pointing at it. The man said he had just seen a ghost standing there and watched it fade away. With that, the maintenance man left as fast as he could, and that was the last anyone ever saw of him at the Evans House!

Joseph told the two women that he was used to hearing mysterious noises and they don't alarm him anymore. In fact, he wasn't scared when he came into work one morning and found what looked like several eight-inch-long bloodstains on the walls.

Could the bloodstains have anything to do with the fact that John Evans was a doctor and Oscar Mahoney was a coroner? Did they leave secrets behind?

The Evans House is not always accessible to the public and is currently used as the home for the Arizona State Historic Preservation Office. Think you're brave enough to volunteer there?

NORTON HOUSE
2700 NORTH FIFTEENTH AVENUE

The grand Norton House was built in 1912 by Dr. James C. Norton, a college professor and veterinarian. James and his wife, Clara, raised their four children—James, Oakley, Victor, and Marietta—on the two-hundred-acre property. The family often played croquet on the big front lawn, and the backyard was filled with fruit tree orchards.

Around 1930, Dr. Norton began selling sections of his property to the City of Phoenix for a new park and golf course. The city finally took over the property in 1935. Today, the Norton House is home to the offices of the Phoenix Parks and Recreation Department.

Debe Branning and a friend visited the property one day, keen to speak with staff who were eager to tell them about the history of the house, as well as some of the mysteries that surround it.

Staff reported that footsteps were often heard on the second floor, and the sounds of children laughing and playing frequently echoed through the house. Once, a maintenance crew member said he saw a woman dressed in an old-fashioned white gown slowly walking across the floor.

Just before Debe and her friend left, the young woman at the front desk remembered something strange that had happened to her. She said there had been a few times when she felt like someone might be in the room, and then suddenly smelled cigar smoke. Smoking isn't allowed in or around the building, so where was the smell coming from?

Even though the Norton family moved out of the house decades ago, it sounds as if they never really left . . .

ELLIS-SHACKELFORD HOUSE
1242 NORTH CENTRAL AVENUE

This historic home was built in 1917 for William C. Ellis, a prominent Phoenix physician. It is located on a part of Central Avenue called "Millionaires' Row" because of all the grand, stately homes that line the street. The Ellis-Shackelford House was placed in the National Register of Historic Places in 1983.

Dr. Ellis's daughter and her husband lived in the house until 1964. Today, the building is owned by the City of Phoenix and the home of Arizona Humanities. Missy Shackelford, the great-granddaughter-in-law of the original owner, works there as an administrative assistant. She says that the family still has ties to the house. And not only because of her job, but because of the ghosts that have hung around! Missy says the ghosts are friendly and peaceful, and it feels like they are being protective. One night, Missy couldn't get the alarm to set. It kept indicating that there was a problem in her office, which also happened to be Uncle Jim Shackelford's old bedroom. Maybe he was playing a trick on her? Was it *also* Uncle Jim causing the sounds of footsteps and doors creaking open and shut that she sometimes heard?

You might think Missy was scared, but in fact, it was just the opposite. She said, "It's very comforting to me. I have a different frame of mind because I knew these 'spirits.' If the 'spirits' are opening doors, I think they're just reminding us that we need to be open and inviting, and we need to bring the community in."

So, if you visit, don't be scared. This house is welcoming to everyone—dead and alive!

Tovrea Castle

Fairy Tale Castles

MYSTERY CASTLE
800 EAST MINERAL ROAD

In the foothills of South Mountain Park is the amazing Mystery Castle. It was built by Boyce Luther Gulley for his beloved daughter, Mary Lou, during the 1930s.

When Mary Lou was young, she loved fairy tales about princes and princesses who lived in castles. At the beach in Seattle, Boyce would create sandcastles for his daughter. When the castles were washed away by the tide, Mary Lou would cry. One day, her father promised he'd build her a castle of her own. He chose to create it in the Arizona desert.

Boyce spent fifteen years building the castle he promised that day. When he died in 1945, it was complete. Mary Lou was no longer a child, but still, she finally had her castle.

A story in *Life* magazine in 1948 gave Boyce Gulley's creation the name "Mystery Castle," and it made Mary Lou and her mother local celebrities.

Mary Lou and her mother needed to find a way to make money to pay for the upkeep of the Mystery Castle, and they decided to give tours of the unusual site. Their Mystery Castle Tours became very popular. Over sixty years later, you can still visit!

The sprawling eighteen-room castle was made of adobe, pieces of steel, glass, and auto parts, has thirteen fireplaces, a chapel, a grotto, and even . . . a dungeon.

But that's not *all* Mystery Castle has. You guessed it, there are also several spirits residing within its walls!

Debe Branning and the MVD Ghostchasers conducted a Paranormal Workshop investigation tour of the Mystery Castle in 2002, and Mary Lou herself gave the tour. She said, "I have seen my father's spirit in the castle many times. He is still protecting myself and the Castle."

Mary Lou also said that late one night, some out-of-town friends decided to pay her a surprise visit, but they ran away when they were chased by some Doberman dogs.

"The funny part was my faithful pair of Dobermans had passed away years before," Mary Lou chuckled. "I believe their animal spirits are still patrolling the grounds."

As Debe and the MVD Ghostchasers made their way through the castle, they passed a staircase leading to an upstairs bedroom. One of the Ghostchasers pointed to the staircase and asked someone to quickly take a photo. She had seen a vision of a man standing on the steps and was hoping it could be caught on camera. The picture didn't reveal anything obvious, but the Ghostchaser was *certain* she'd seen a ghost. Was it the spirit of Boyce Gulley?

Mary Lou passed away in 2010 at the age of eighty. The castle is on the Arizona Registry of Historic Places. Visitors can sign up online for daytime tours or join in on an occasional nighttime paranormal investigation. Which would you choose? Day or night?

TOVREA CASTLE
5025 EAST VAN BUREN STREET

Alessio Carraro was an Italian immigrant who traveled to Phoenix in 1928 and had a vision of building a luxury resort hotel surrounded by a beautiful cactus garden. The hotel never materialized, however, Carraro did build a unique architectural structure now known as Tovrea Castle. Many locals refer to it as the "Wedding Cake House" because of its unusual shape.

Alessio completed the stunning building in 1931, but unfortunately, he couldn't afford to live there. He put the property up for sale, and it was purchased by Edward A. Tovrea, a local cattle baron.

Edward died of pneumonia in 1932, and his wife, Della, remarried in 1936. Della and her new husband, Stuart, lived near Prescott during the summers and in the castle during the winter. Stuart died of natural causes in 1960. Both Edward and Stuart died at the castle, adding to the mystery over the years.

Della died in 1969, and eventually, the castle fell into disrepair. In 1993, the City of Phoenix purchased Tovrea Castle and started renovating the structure. Over the years, it has since become one of Phoenix's popular tourist attractions.

One of the tour guides recounted how he once heard giggling and the sound of a ball bouncing in the house. When he went to investigate where the sound was coming from, there was no one there. And it's said that a workman once found a child's footprint in a pile of sawdust when there were definitely no children on the site.

Della had no children of her own, but she had several nieces and nephews who came to visit. Maybe one of these children had come back in the afterlife, hoping to relive happier times at the castle?

Are you brave enough to pay a visit and perhaps make a new ghostly friend?

A Ghostly Goodbye

Did you enjoy discovering the spooky side of Phoenix? Or were you hiding under the covers as you read? Ultimately, it's up to you to decide what you think about the eerie events that happen in the city nicknamed Valley of the Sun. Are the apparitions and noises real or just imagined? Whether you live in Phoenix or are just visiting, one thing's for sure—there seem to be plenty of ghosts who call this city home. And, just like the Phoenix bird, more ghosts will surely rise to tell their tales. We've only just begun to meet the spirits who reside there . . .

New York Times bestselling author **STACIA DEUTSCH** has written more than three hundred children's books, including *The Jessie Files,* a spin-off of the beloved *Boxcar Children* mystery series. Stacia lives in Temecula, California, where she is a member of the historical society. She loves hearing spooky stories! Find her at www.staciadeutsch.com, on Instagram @staciadeutsch_writes, and www.facebook.com/staciadeutsch.

Check out some of the other *Spooky America* titles available now!

   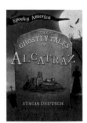

 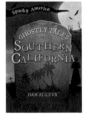  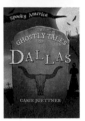

   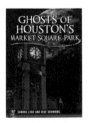

Spooky America was adapted from the creeptastic *Haunted America* series for adults. *Haunted America* explores historical haunts in cities and regions across America. Here's more from the original *Haunted Phoenix* author, Debe Branning: